I0791016

Living With You

© 2015

Living With You
Story of an Orphaned Raccoon

By Robin C. Kocher
Illustrated by James A. Brown

Special thanks to
Jane Swartz and Brandi McCormick
for their help in editing this book

This book is dedicated to wildlife orphans,

and the wonderful people who care for them.

Proceeds from this book go toward food, shelter and other supplies needed to care for and rehabilitate orphaned and injured wildlife.

In memory of James Antonio Brown

May your artwork be an inspiration to us all.

The Story Teller

Illustration by: Brandi McCormick

I am Houston, the family cat. I would like to share a story with you about a wild orphan that would not have survived apart from the compassion of those who found and cared for her.

People that dedicate their time caring for others make our world a more beautiful place to live. I know, because I was an orphan myself once, and someone took me in and cared for me.

Our story begins in the western part of America, and took place years ago in a quiet suburb, which is a unique place on the boundary where people and wildlife often live in the same spaces.

One morning in the early spring, Dog and I were walking in the woods with Sara. On our way home, a neighbor called us to come over to her yard. She sounded concerned, so we went over to see what was wrong. Sadly, Jayne had found a dead raccoon lying on the floor of her shed.

As the ladies were talking a faint chattering sound was

heard inside the shed. Sara and Jayne found where the sound was coming from, and there shivering on the cold floor was a baby raccoon, barely able to crawl. Sara found some gloves picked the baby up and took her inside.

"What should we do? Who can we call?" I heard Jayne ask. "Who can take care of this baby raccoon?"

Jayne and Sara made several calls and discovered the sad truth about what happens to  many orphaned wildlife. Most baby animals are taken and destroyed by the authorities.

One person they spoke with told them about kind people called 

"Rehabilitators," who are trained to care for orphaned wildlife, but very few people volunteer for this job and there was no one available in our area.

Realizing they were the only hope the baby had, Jayne went and found an electric blanket, and the baby girl curled up into the warmth and quickly fell asleep. From that day on, I decided to call her Girly.

In the beginning, Girly was too small to eat regular food, and   needed to be bottle fed many times, both day and night.

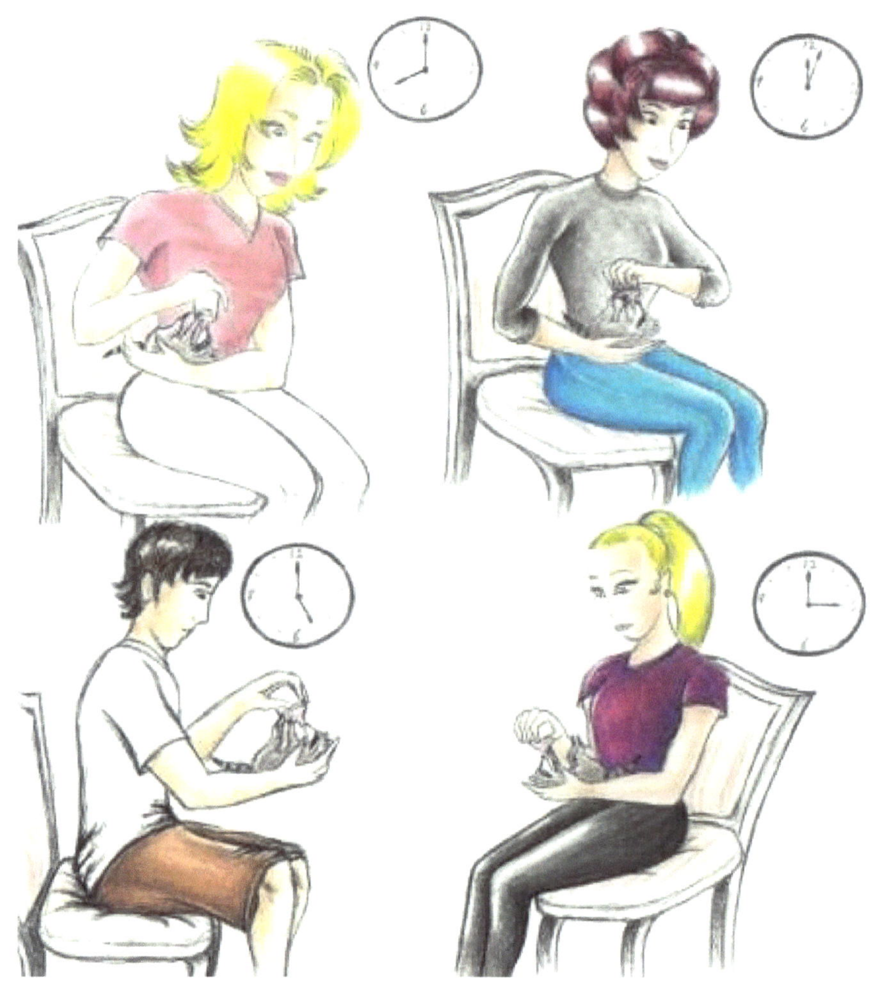

Bottle feedings went on for several weeks. It seemed like a lot of work, but everyone helped, including two teenagers named Adam and Hollister. I found it strange that a baby raccoon enjoyed kitten formula so much. When I was a baby I didn't care for it much!

Girly was very small and unable to walk at first, but as the weeks and months passed by she grew and became more active. She developed a natural hunch in her back and her hair grew longer and thicker. She had very strong legs, and agile hands.

I was wise to have kept her in place from the beginning. She learned that I was king in the house, and she must not mess with me.

Although Girly did not battle me, she enjoyed a good match with her arch enemy, a puppet named Panda Bear.

She would leap into the air to meet his attack, wrestling him to the ground, then biting him all over. He was quite a mess when she got through with him. Even though Panda Bear was just a puppet, I think it helped Girly develop fighting skills she might need one day.

In early summer when the leaves came out and she was able to keep up, Sara let Girly join us outside for our morning walks.

After we finished our business, we would play in the woods. We all enjoyed this time together. I was surprised that Girly could climb trees at such a young age. Sometimes she would climb so high you could barely see her.

Girly and I climbed trees together. I tried to show off my climbing skills to her, but I discovered she had skills of her own. Not only could she climb higher and better than me, she could come down head first. Her hind legs could pivot backwards, allowing her a strong hugging grip on the tree. I wouldn't dare try that because I would fall on my face. I am careful and climb down backwards slowly.

As for Dog he can't climb at all!

Girly was not like Dog or me,
she was more like a monkey-cat.

She may have been a wild animal, but her cleverness and
physical abilities allowed her to interact with Sara in ways
that Dog and I could not. I think they had fun teasing and
playing with each other.

Every morning after our walk, we would meet in the kitchen for breakfast. I always got breakfast first because I am the most important. I get hard food with tuna fish on top. Girly liked bananas and grapes, but her favorite food was eggs.

And, every day Dog jumped up and down when he saw his breakfast coming.

Girly often got special attention since she was so young and cried at night. Do you know she was allowed to sleep on Sara's bed, but Dog and I were not. That's Ok, Sara doesn't know it, but Dog and I both get on her bed when she's not looking.

Girly was actually very gentle in the mornings when she first woke up. She would use her hands and fingers to softly open Sara's eyes.   I think it was her way of saying "Good morning, time to wake up."   Living with her was often filled with unique and unexpected moments.

Sometimes during the day, I would act like I was sleeping and tease her with my tail, waving it back and forth. She tried to catch it, and I pretended not to notice.

Nothing was safe from her snooping, she would inspect everything! She would even lift Dog's ear and look in it.

And without fail, everyday she opened the shower drain to stick her hand into the muck.

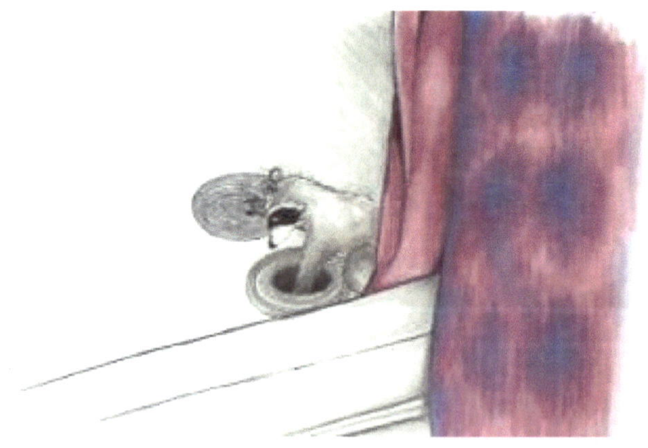

Out of all the rooms in the house Girly liked the bathroom best.

When no one could find her, she was often asleep in the trashcan or playing under the sink, investigating all the interesting stuff people use, like cotton swabs, shampoo and toilet paper.

She was always acting silly, always on the move, and no one ever knew where she might show up next. Her favorite game seemed to be hide and seek.

When Sara took a shower, Girly thought she was trying to hide from her, so she would reach her hands under the curtain feeling around for Sara's toes. Now that made Sara laugh!

There was a trust between Sara and Girly, and they shared an interest in learning about one another. Sometimes they looked closely at one another investigating each other's features.

Her sense of touch seemed very important to her discovery process. Girly had hands much like a human, but no chin what-so-ever. She had a strong curiosity about ears, and was always poking her finger in them.

As for Dog and me, we prefer to use our noses and sense of smell instead.

Even though we all liked Girly, she continued to get into things, and sometimes she could really make a big mess.

As the days passed I think Sara began to see why Girly could not be a pet like Dog and me. She needed a different type of life where she could be free to be her wild self.

Bedtime was often not as peaceful as mornings were, because Girly was a nocturnal animal and nighttime was her most active part of the day. She became quite a little beast at times desperately wanting to play-fight with Sara.

Sometimes she would attack Sara's hair pulling and biting at it.

Sara would hide under the covers to get away from her, and Girly would try to get in.

Well, good morning you little stinker!

I take it you got some sleep?

One summer day, I heard Sara talking to Girly. She
seemed sad and concerned, so I moved closer to listen.
I heard her say that Girly was not like Dog and me, and
that she was really from the woods outside, and that was
her real home.

She was
afraid to
let her go
because
there
may not
be
enough
food or
space for
her to
live in the
small
woods
near our
home,
and if she
got
hungry
and got
into
people's
garbage cans, they would not like that.

Sara's other fear of letting Girly go was that most
people do not understand or care about raccoons, so
they want to get rid of them, and some people even kill
them.

Then, one evening in late summer while Girly and I were playing, a strange animal came to the backdoor, and it sat there watching us through the glass.

Girly was very curious about the visitor, because it looked just like her - only bigger. The next thing I knew she had slipped out the door following right behind the other raccoon. And just like that, she was gone.

I wonder sometimes if I should have made her stay.

I know it was difficult for Sara to watch her go. She had become like a mother to the young raccoon and loved her very much.   Although she knew there were dangers outside for Girly, Sara also knew it was the right thing to let her go and live her life with the other raccoons.

As Sara watched her disappear into the night I heard her whisper, "I am going to miss you little girl. You made my life more beautiful - caring for you."

Glossary

Agile - able to move quickly and easily

Authorities - the power or right to give orders, make decisions, and enforce obedience

Formula - manufactured food designed and marketed for feeding to babies, usually prepared for bottle-feeding from powder (mixed with water) or liquid (with or without additional water).

Hunch - Raise or bend into a hump

Nocturnal - occurring, or active at night

Orphan - a child whose parents are dead or have permanently abandoned the child

Rehabilitator – a person who restores an animal to a condition of good health, and helps them learn to survive in the wild

Suburb - an outlying district of a city, especially a residential one

**"What should we do with her? Who can we call ?"
"Who can take care of this baby?"**

When wildlife babies are found alone the
mother may be near, so unless you are
sure the animal is orphaned or injured it is
always best to leave it alone.

If you do find an orphaned or injured wild animal and you want
to provide care always use caution. It is wise to use gloves and
place the animal in a cage. Give the animal a warm, dark and
quiet place to rest until you can get further assistance by a
licensed wildlife rehabilitator. Warmth may be the most
important thing you can provide to an injured or baby animal,
and the dark quietness will help to reduce stress.

To learn more about what you can do to help orphaned
wildlife, or become a volunteer rehabilitator in your area
contact your local Department of Natural Resources and ask
for information about your state's Wildlife Rehabilitator
Program. Or contact:

The National Wildlife Rehabilitators Association
Website: http://www.nwrawildlife.org/
Phone: NWRA at (320) 230-9920

**Various states in the US have different laws concerning the
care of orphaned and injured wildlife, and those laws are
subject to change. For your own protection, it is helpful to
know about your state's wildlife laws and the reasons for
them.**

About

Robin Kocher MA.Ed.

Robin is a mother of four wonderful children – the pride and joy of her life. She holds a Bachelors degree in Geology and a Masters in Education. Over the years she has served as an environmental technician, science teacher, and social advocate.

A note from the author

James Brown was a polite and gentle, talented young man I met while volunteering as a tutor at the men's homeless shelter in Cleveland, OH. James had hoped to obtain his GED to create a better life for himself. This would not be easy because James struggled with a learning disability. James also had a heart condition which prevented him from physically demanding work.

James Antonio Brown

James joined me as the illustrator for this book and over the course of a year we became good friends. His creative talent brought this story to life. All his images were drawn in pen and colored with pencils. He greatly desired to escape poverty, to be appreciated and to be loved. We lost this special young man to his heart condition in the spring of 2017.

Never believe that a few caring people
can't change the world. For, indeed,
that's all who ever have.

Margaret Mead